A FORGIVENESS WORKBOOK

BARBARA J. MURCHISON GRADY

WestBow
PRESS®
A DIVISION OF THOMAS NELSON
& ZONDERVAN

WestBow Press books may be ordered through booksellers or by contacting:

WestBow Press
A Division of Thomas Nelson & Zondervan
1663 Liberty Drive
Bloomington, IN 47403
www.westbowpress.com
1 (866) 928-1240

Because of the dynamic nature of the Internet, any web addresses or links contained in
this book may have changed since publication and may no longer be valid. The views
expressed in this work are solely those of the author and do not necessarily reflect the views
of the publisher, and the publisher hereby disclaims any responsibility for them.

Scripture quotations marked NKJV are taken from the New King James Version®.
Copyright © 1982 by Thomas Nelson. Used by permission. All rights reserved.

Scripture quotations marked NIV are taken from The Holy Bible, New International Version®, NIV®
Copyright © 1973, 1978, 1984, 2011 by Biblica, Inc.® Used by permission. All rights reserved worldwide.

Any people depicted in stock imagery provided by Getty Images are models,
and such images are being used for illustrative purposes only.
Certain stock imagery © Getty Images.

ISBN: 978-1-9736-6800-8 (sc)
ISBN: 978-1-9736-6801-5 (e)

Print information available on the last page.

WestBow Press rev. date: 07/08/2019

What is forgiveness?

How do I forgive?

That seems impossible. Lord, I don't want to forgive. Lord, help me to forgive.

I want to forgive.

To the God of my salvation, I honor You.

I have written this workbook as a directive from Him.

The Lord, Jesus Christ

Contents

Preface

To every person—man, woman, boy, or girl—to the young, old, and in between, the purpose of this workbook is to provide a simple, hands-on approach to forgiveness.

There is no condemnation for anyone. However, I believe this workbook will help lift you to the next level. You may ask, "What is the next level?" It can be the next level of healing, deliverance, or freedom.

My prayer, my aim, my goal is to help relieve you of any pain you have in your life, be it mental or emotional pain. May God, our heavenly Father, release you from any mental or emotional bondage you may have.

God bless as you work His Word in your life.

Introduction

God, our heavenly Father, and our Lord, Jesus Christ, are the great forgivers of all time. From the Old Testament to the New Testament, Genesis to Revelation, our great God of holiness is our forgiver.

It is His nature to love, discipline us when or if it is needed, and forgive. He also commands that we love, walk according to His Word, and forgive. He wants us to imitate Him.

God forgives iniquity and transgression and sin

> Exodus 34:5–7
> Proverbs 3:12

Jesus forgives and cleanse

> St. John 8:11; 15:3
> 1 John 1:9

We must forgive

> Matthew 18:21–22
> St. Luke 17:1–4

Chapter 1

LIFE

Many things can happen to a person in this life. A person can do many things during his or her lifetime.

There are so many experiences, each with different dynamics and variables, that it is hard to contend with them. As a result of situations that have happened in your life, you may be struggling about what to do. You may wonder, *"How can I escape?"* God has provided a way of escape for all His children. Sometimes you just have to forgive. There is a saying by Alexander Pope that goes like this: "To error is human, to forgive is divine." Talk to the Lord about it, and let Him handle it. That is the great escape.

When we forgive a person for any offense, the following occurs.

- It will untie God's hands to work in a situation. If we try to take matters into our own hands without acknowledging Him or His Word, we can make things worse.
- It will benefit us. We obey God and become free in our minds, hearts, emotions, and bodies. Our thoughts can affect our emotions, and our emotions can affect our bodies to where we become physically sick.
- It will set us free to live out our lives in peace. In the midst of a storm inside or out, forgiveness from our hearts (our innermost beings) brings a great calm.

No matter who or what it is, make the decision to forgive. In the Old Testament, God commands us to forgive. In the New Testament, Jesus Christ, God's Son, taught and practiced forgiveness. Oh, how He forgave and continues to forgive us!

There are many scriptures on forgiveness. Let's talk about a few of them.

In Matthew 18:21–22, Peter asked Jesus how often he should forgive his brother. Should it be seven times? Jesus said not seven times but seven times seventy. The subject is revisited in Luke 17:1–4. I encourage you to read both passages a few times and then think about them.

In Luke 17:1 (NKJV), it says,

> Then He said to his disciples,
>
> "It is impossible that no offenses should come, but woe to him through whom they do come!
>
> It would be better for him if a millstone were hung around his neck and he were thrown into the sea, than that he should offend one of these little ones.
>
> Take heed to yourselves. If your brother sins against you, rebuke him; and if he repents, forgive him.
>
> And if he sins against you seven times in a day, and seven times in a day returns to you, saying, 'I repent,' you shall forgive him."

In the very next verse, Luke 17:5, the apostles said to the Lord, "Increase our faith." I understand the apostles. I think you do too.

As for me, I used to think if I needed to forgive a person seven times in one day or 490 times, something was wrong with that person. "Call the men with the white coats. He or she needs to be institutionalized."

Nevertheless, God told me to forgive from my heart. When I forgive from my heart, it does not hurt anymore. When I forgive from my heart, the offense fades from my mind. When I forgive from my heart, if or when I talk about it or share the experience with someone, I do not get heated or irritated. I can look at the situation more objectively. When all these points line up for me, I have reached the desired results.

One Sunday morning, May 20, 2012, my pastor talked to the congregation about forgiveness. I felt I had forgiven and didn't hold anything against anybody. I was fine. But in the midddle of the message, hurt flooded my mind and emotions.

When I got home, I prayed within myself in a quiet voice, *"Lord, I am so sorry I have not overcome this thing like You want me to."*

There was a quick response. "Forgive from your heart."

Then I said, "Lord, I thought I had done that."

Immediately, this portion of scripture came: "Seven times seventy."

I wondered, *How do you do that?* The next thought hit my mind: *Write it down.*

Sometimes you have to forgive by faith. Say it with your mouth, or write it down. Even though you do not feel it, you are setting forgiveness in motion. After that, walk through it.

Before and after dinner, I went to my prayer room and started to write down who had offended me and the date I started this process. It took me three days to complete it, but I did what the Lord told the prophet to do. In Habakkuk 2:2, the Lord said, "Write the vision and make it plain upon tables, that he may run that read it."

This Sunday morning message from my pastor, a prayer of repentance, and an instruction from the Spirit of God happened in one afternoon. After finishing the task of writing things down, I can say I am free. There will be many opportunities to practice forgiveness. When I face a new trial, if it is heavy-duty, I start the process again until I reach the desired results.

Chapter 2

THE INSTRUCTION

Over a period of three years, I talked about what the Lord showed me about working through things that seemed hard.

While standing in worship on October 7, 2015, during the Wednesday night prayer service, I had a strong desire and a heavy thought to write a workbook on forgiveness. A little while later, my pastor asked us to wait and be quiet before the Lord to hear what He would speak to us. So the thought came back. It flooded my mind.

Well, I thought, *I need conformation.* The reason I needed conformation is I've never wanted to write a book of any kind. It's a good thing for someone else but not for me. In my mind, there are enough good books on the subject. Nevertheless, I must obey.

One of my friends told me about a family situation that hurt her and her siblings. She was not bitter, but the thought of the situation brought pain. We talked about the exercise the Lord gave me. She tried the process, and before completion, the burden and pain lifted off her.

Writing things down is a natural physical exercise with a spiritual application because it requires you to think and feel and tell God about it.

For some people, writing things down is so elementary that it is an insult to their intellects. But remember 1 Corinthians 1:18–21. Preaching the gospel is foolishness to the unbelievers, but they come to Christ and get saved. So this simple exercise may confound you.

> For the message of the cross is foolishness to those who are perishing, but to us who are being saved it is the power of God.

> For since, in the wisdom of God, the world through wisdom did not know God, it pleased God through the foolishness of the message preached to save those who believe. (1 Corinthians 1:18, 21 NKJV)

Chapter 3

DEFINITIONS AND A LIST OF THINGS

As we approach the process, the definition of "forgiveness" is to pardon. "To pardon" means to release the offense and offender from further punishment. To forgive means to give up resentment against or the desire to punish. It means to let the person off the hook, especially off your hook.

Below is a short list of situations that can cause wounds, bruises, and offenses. There are some unimaginable atrocities a person may experience that I can't name, but I hope this list will motivate you to action and still be a blessing for you to ponder about your future. What are you going to do?

- An abusive parent
- A compulsive liar
- Divorce
- An abusive husband or wife
- A rebellious son or daughter
- A broken relationship with a family member or friend
- Conflict or harassment on your job
- A loved one who was killed or murdered
- False accusations
- An attempt to destroy your influence or reputation
- Being a victim of rape
- Mean people (church bullies, school bullies, and so on)

- Obnoxious neighbors
- A controller
- A manipulator
- A person who practices witchcraft
- A thief (something stolen from you)
- Someone leading you astray
- Someone acting like he or she is better than you
- Someone with a substance abuse problem (drugs and/or alcohol)
- A cold, unfeeling person
- A critical person
- A self-righteous Christian
- An adulterer
- A family member who gambles away finances

Chapter 4

THE PROCESS

Before you start the process, pray. And during the process, pray. Talk honestly and earnestly to God. Pour out your heart to Him. Trust Him like you would a best friend with what's going on with you. Take your time, and think about what happened. Walk through the hurt, anger, or insult, yet forgive.

Do not be afraid or ashamed to express your emotions or how you feel before Him. The Lord knows anyway. There are those who would say, "Do not go before God with all that stuff." I am not advocating bellyaching. I am talking about coming before our Father and being honest with Him.

There may be a time when you come in contact with people who live in never-never land. They have never spoken, felt, seen, heard, smelled, or touched anything. Everything is just great. When you meet a person like that, *run!*

I encourage you to be transparent before almighty God because He loves, cares for, and wants to hear from you. If you need to, cry. I mean shed real tears. Remember, Jesus cried over Jerusalem (Luke 19:11) and at Lazarus's grave (John 11:35).

If you are angry about something, tell Him. Just don't sin by falsely accusing Him, like I have in the past of something He did not do. After doing that, I had to backtrack and straighten out my words, asking Him to forgive and help me.

Jesus was upset with the money changers in His house. The account is recorded in all four gospels: Matthew 21:12, Mark 11:15, Luke 19:45, and John 2:13–17. I am pointing this out because Christ Jesus is our High Priest, and He can be touched by, understand the feelings of our infirmities (whatever ails you). We serve the only God who has emotions. He is a talking, seeing, hearing, thinking, touching, feeling God.

When you can think and articulate what you are feeling (hurt, pain, anger), you are digging up, cleaning out, and throwing away the root cause of unforgiveness. As you write the person's name down, think, feel, and say to God, "I forgive."

Now, let the cleansing, healing, forgiving process begin. God bless as you start.

Date _____

Lord, You said forgive seven times seventy (7 × 70).
Be sure to write the person's name.

1.   I forgive_____

2.   I forgive_____

3.   I forgive_____

4.   I forgive_____

5.   I forgive_____

6.   I forgive_____

7.   I forgive_____

8.   I forgive_____

9.   I forgive_____

10.   I forgive_____

11.   I forgive_____

12.   I forgive_____

13.   I forgive_____

14.   I forgive_____

15.   I forgive_____

16.   I forgive_____

17.   I forgive_____

18.   I forgive_____

19.   I forgive_____

20. I forgive_____

21. I forgive_____

22. I forgive_____

23. I forgive_____

24. I forgive_____

25. I forgive_____

26. I forgive_____

27. I forgive_____

28. I forgive_____

29. I forgive_____

30. I forgive_____

31. I forgive_____

32. I forgive_____

33. I forgive_____

34. I forgive_____

35. I forgive_____

36. I forgive_____

37. I forgive_____

38. I forgive_____

39. I forgive_____

40. I forgive_____

41. I forgive_____

42. I forgive_____

43. I forgive_____

44. I forgive_____

45. I forgive_____

46. I forgive_____

47. I forgive_____

48. I forgive_____

49. I forgive_____

50. I forgive_____

51. I forgive_____

52. I forgive_____

53. I forgive_____

54. I forgive_____

55. I forgive_____

56. I forgive_____

57. I forgive_____

58. I forgive_____

59. I forgive_____

60. I forgive_____

61. I forgive_____

62. I forgive_____

63. I forgive_____

64. I forgive_____

65. I forgive_____

66. I forgive_____

67. I forgive_____

68. I forgive_____

69. I forgive_____

70. I forgive_____

71. I forgive_____

72. I forgive_____

73. I forgive_____

74. I forgive_____

75. I forgive_____

76. I forgive_____

77. I forgive_____

78. I forgive_____

79. I forgive_____

80. I forgive_____

81. I forgive_____

82. I forgive_____

83. I forgive_____

84. I forgive_____

85. I forgive_____

86. I forgive_____

87. I forgive_____

88. I forgive_____

89. I forgive_____

90. I forgive_____

91. I forgive_____

92. I forgive_____

93. I forgive_____

94. I forgive_____

95. I forgive_____

96. I forgive_____

97. I forgive_____

98. I forgive_____

99. I forgive_____

100. I forgive_____

101. I forgive_____

102. I forgive_____

103. I forgive_____

104. I forgive_____

105. I forgive_____

106. I forgive_____

107. I forgive_____

108. I forgive_____

109. I forgive_____

110. I forgive_____

111. I forgive_____

112. I forgive_____

113. I forgive_____

114. I forgive_____

115. I forgive_____

116. I forgive_____

117. I forgive_____

118. I forgive_____

119. I forgive_____

120. I forgive_____

121. I forgive_____

122. I forgive_____

123. I forgive_____

124. I forgive_____

125. I forgive_____

126. I forgive_____

127. I forgive_____

128. I forgive_____

129. I forgive_____

130. I forgive_____

131. I forgive_____

132. I forgive_____

133. I forgive_____

134. I forgive_____

135. I forgive_____

136. I forgive_____

137. I forgive_____

138. I forgive_____

139. I forgive_____

140. I forgive_____

141. I forgive_____

142. I forgive_____

143. I forgive_____

144. I forgive_____

145. I forgive_____

146. I forgive_____

147. I forgive_____

148. I forgive_____

149. I forgive_____

150. I forgive_____

151. I forgive_____

152. I forgive _____

153. I forgive _____

154. I forgive _____

155. I forgive _____

156. I forgive _____

157. I forgive _____

158. I forgive _____

159. I forgive _____

160. I forgive _____

161. I forgive _____

162. I forgive _____

163. I forgive _____

164. I forgive _____

165. I forgive _____

166. I forgive _____

167. I forgive _____

168. I forgive _____

169. I forgive _____

170. I forgive _____

171. I forgive _____

172. I forgive _____

173. I forgive _____

174. I forgive_____

175. I forgive_____

176. I forgive_____

177. I forgive_____

178. I forgive_____

179. I forgive_____

180. I forgive_____

181. I forgive_____

182. I forgive_____

183. I forgive_____

184. I forgive_____

185. I forgive_____

186. I forgive_____

187. I forgive_____

188. I forgive_____

189. I forgive_____

190. I forgive_____

191. I forgive_____

192. I forgive_____

193. I forgive_____

194. I forgive_____

195. I forgive_____

196. I forgive_____

197. I forgive_____

198. I forgive_____

199. I forgive_____

200. I forgive_____

201. I forgive_____

202. I forgive_____

203. I forgive_____

204. I forgive_____

205. I forgive_____

206. I forgive_____

207. I forgive_____

208. I forgive_____

209. I forgive_____

210. I forgive_____

211. I forgive_____

212. I forgive_____

213. I forgive_____

214. I forgive_____

215. I forgive_____

216. I forgive_____

217. I forgive_____

218. I forgive_____

219. I forgive_____

220. I forgive_____

221. I forgive_____

222. I forgive_____

223. I forgive_____

224. I forgive_____

225. I forgive_____

226. I forgive_____

227. I forgive_____

228. I forgive_____

229. I forgive_____

230. I forgive_____

231. I forgive_____

232. I forgive_____

233. I forgive_____

234. I forgive_____

235. I forgive_____

236. I forgive_____

237. I forgive_____

238. I forgive_____

239. I forgive_____

240. I forgive_____

241. I forgive_____

242. I forgive_____

243. I forgive_____

244. I forgive_____

245. I forgive_____

246. I forgive_____

247. I forgive_____

248. I forgive_____

249. I forgive_____

250. I forgive_____

251. I forgive_____

252. I forgive_____

253. I forgive_____

254. I forgive_____

255. I forgive_____

256. I forgive_____

257. I forgive_____

258. I forgive_____

259. I forgive_____

260. I forgive_____

261. I forgive_____

262. I forgive_____

263. I forgive_____

264. I forgive_____

265. I forgive_____

266. I forgive_____

267. I forgive_____

268. I forgive_____

269. I forgive_____

270. I forgive_____

271. I forgive_____

272. I forgive_____

273. I forgive_____

274. I forgive_____

275. I forgive_____

276. I forgive_____

277. I forgive_____

278. I forgive_____

279. I forgive_____

280. I forgive_____

281. I forgive_____

282. I forgive_____

283. I forgive_____

284. I forgive_____

285. I forgive_____

286. I forgive_____

287. I forgive_____

288. I forgive_____

289. I forgive_____

290. I forgive_____

291. I forgive_____

292. I forgive_____

293. I forgive_____

294. I forgive_____

295. I forgive_____

296. I forgive_____

297. I forgive_____

298. I forgive_____

299. I forgive_____

300. I forgive_____

301. I forgive_____

302. I forgive_____

303. I forgive_____

304. I forgive_____

305. I forgive_____

306. I forgive_____

307. I forgive_____

308. I forgive_____

309. I forgive_____

310. I forgive_____

311. I forgive_____

312. I forgive_____

313. I forgive_____

314. I forgive_____

315. I forgive_____

316. I forgive_____

317. I forgive_____

318. I forgive_____

319. I forgive_____

320. I forgive_____

321. I forgive_____

322. I forgive_____

323. I forgive_____

324. I forgive_____

325. I forgive_____

326. I forgive_____

327. I forgive_____

328. I forgive_____

329. I forgive_____

330. I forgive_____

331. I forgive_____

332. I forgive_____

333. I forgive_____

334. I forgive_____

335. I forgive_____

336. I forgive_____

337. I forgive_____

338. I forgive_____

339. I forgive_____

340. I forgive_____

341. I forgive_____

342. I forgive_____

343. I forgive_____

344. I forgive_____

345. I forgive_____

346. I forgive_____

347. I forgive_____

348. I forgive_____

349. I forgive_____

350. I forgive_____

351. I forgive_____

352. I forgive_____

353. I forgive_____

354. I forgive_____

355. I forgive_____

356. I forgive_____

357. I forgive_____

358. I forgive_____

359. I forgive_____

360. I forgive_____

361. I forgive_____

362. I forgive_____

363. I forgive_____

364. I forgive_____

365. I forgive_____

366. I forgive_____

367. I forgive_____

368. I forgive_____

369. I forgive_____

370. I forgive_____

371. I forgive_____

372. I forgive _____

373. I forgive _____

374. I forgive _____

375. I forgive _____

376. I forgive _____

377. I forgive _____

378. I forgive _____

379. I forgive _____

380. I forgive _____

381. I forgive _____

382. I forgive _____

383. I forgive _____

384. I forgive _____

385. I forgive _____

386. I forgive _____

387. I forgive _____

388. I forgive _____

389. I forgive _____

390. I forgive _____

391. I forgive _____

392. I forgive _____

393. I forgive _____

394. I forgive_____

395. I forgive_____

396. I forgive_____

397. I forgive_____

398. I forgive_____

399. I forgive_____

400. I forgive_____

401. I forgive_____

402. I forgive_____

403. I forgive_____

404. I forgive_____

405. I forgive_____

406. I forgive_____

407. I forgive_____

408. I forgive_____

409. I forgive_____

410. I forgive_____

411. I forgive_____

412. I forgive_____

413. I forgive_____

414. I forgive_____

415. I forgive_____

416. I forgive_____

417. I forgive_____

418. I forgive_____

419. I forgive_____

420. I forgive_____

421. I forgive_____

422. I forgive_____

423. I forgive_____

424. I forgive_____

425. I forgive_____

426. I forgive_____

427. I forgive_____

428. I forgive_____

429. I forgive_____

430. I forgive_____

431. I forgive_____

432. I forgive_____

433. I forgive_____

434. I forgive_____

435. I forgive_____

436. I forgive_____

437. I forgive_____

438. I forgive_____

439. I forgive_____

440. I forgive_____

441. I forgive_____

442. I forgive_____

443. I forgive_____

444. I forgive_____

445. I forgive_____

446. I forgive_____

447. I forgive_____

448. I forgive_____

449. I forgive_____

450. I forgive_____

451. I forgive_____

452. I forgive_____

453. I forgive_____

454. I forgive_____

455. I forgive_____

456. I forgive_____

457. I forgive_____

458. I forgive_____

459. I forgive_____

460. I forgive_____

461. I forgive_____

462. I forgive_____

463. I forgive_____

464. I forgive_____

465. I forgive_____

466. I forgive_____

467. I forgive_____

468. I forgive_____

469. I forgive_____

470. I forgive_____

471. I forgive_____

472. I forgive_____

473. I forgive_____

474. I forgive_____

475. I forgive_____

476. I forgive_____

477. I forgive_____

478. I forgive_____

479. I forgive_____

480. I forgive_____

481. I forgive_____

482. I forgive_____

483. I forgive_____

484. I forgive_____

485. I forgive_____

486. I forgive_____

487. I forgive_____

488. I forgive_____

489. I forgive_____

490. I forgive_____

Now that you have completed the process, write a prayer of victory.

Lord Jesus, I have forgiven according to Your Word. I thank You for helping me.

_____

_____

_____

_____

_____

Chapter 5

REFLECTIONS

Sometimes, forgiving someone can be hard. There are several factors to consider. It depends on:

- Who offended you.
- What the offense was.
- When the offense happened.
- Where the offense happened.
- Why the offense happened.
- How the offense happened.

There are two types of offenders: the unintentional offender and the deliberate, intentional offender. The unintentional offender is easier to forgive because in that person's heart, no hurt or harm is meant. He or she may say something or act in a way that is improper toward you. After the offense, the person may apologize, say, "I am sorry. Forgive me. I meant no harm."

James 3:2 says we all trip and stumble over different things. But the person who does not offend with words is a perfect or mature person and able to keep his or her whole body under control. This scripture tells me if I can keep from offending anybody with my words, through Christ, I will be able to control my body, mind, will, and emotions. If you can control what you say by not condemning and prejudging with bitter words, you can keep yourself from unnecessary attacks. If you will be swift to hear, slow to speak, and slow to get angry, you will be able to escape many things.

This has been my prayer for many years: "Lord, set a watch over my mouth, so I don't sin with my tongue." In other words, help me not to say things I have no business saying.

The deliberate, intentional offender can have an offensive attitude and stance. This type of person can be obnoxious and insulting, thinking he or she has been given the right to behave in this way. This offender will think about it, plan it, tell someone about it, and then carry out the offense. Acting in this manner can cause outrage to the senses. It is an assault that can cause hurt, anger, resentment, and displeasure.

How do you forgive such a person? You must forgive by faith, asking the Lord to help you. As time passes, your heart will soften, and you will be able to pray for the person's well-being. This type person may never admit any wrongdoing or mistakes. You may not be able to talk or reason with the person. Turn the situation over to the Lord. He knows how to reach all of us. After that, be determined to move forward to obey His Word.

The Lord has great plans for you and me and me and you. Read what He said in Jeremiah 29:11 (KJV): "For I know the thoughts that I think toward you, saith the Lord, thoughts of peace, and not of evil, to give you an expected end."

The NIV Bible says it like this: "For I know the plans I have for you, declares the Lord, "plans to prosper you and not to harm you, plans to give you hope and a future."

Our God is the only God who can do that for us. To possess His promises, we have to forgive.

Chapter 6

FINAL WORD

To engage in this exercise is not a commandment. To forgive is commandment. Read the Word of the Lord. This is what Jesus said in Matthew 6:14–15 (NKJV):

> For if you forgive men their trespasses, your heavenly Father will also forgive you. But if you do not forgive men their trespasses, neither will your Father forgive your trespasses.

You may have a different approach on how to handle forgiveness, and that's okay. I encourage you to obey His Word.

Jesus said, "If your brother sins against you, rebuke him. If he repents forgive him" (Luke 17:3 NKJV). Jesus also said, "Go to your brother alone, … Take one or two with you, … take the situation before the church" (Matthew 18:15–17 NKJV).

There may be a time that neither of these instructions occurs. It may depend on the magnitude of the offense. Time will resolve some issues. Nevertheless, you still have to forgive.

Forgiveness is not letting someone get away with something. It's not just letting them off the hook. I repeat, it's letting them off your hook. Put them on God's hook. God can and will deal with a person as He sees fit.

Once you go through the stages of forgiveness you may still need prayer. Go to a good man or woman of God. Go to a Christian friend who knows how to pray. "Confess your faults one to another, and prayer for one another, that you may be healed" (James 5:16 KJV). Notice it does not say confess your faults to the whole world but to one another.

As we pray for each other, learn to walk in forgiveness. Christ will be seen in our lives, and we can live out our lives in peace.

May God richly bless and keep you this day and in the days to come.

Printed in the United States
By Bookmasters